THE LITTLE

BOOK OF

NOSTRADAMUS

Prophecies for the
21st Century

HERBIE BRENNAN

Thorsons
An Imprint of HarperCollins*Publishers*
77–85 Fulham Palace Road,
Hammersmith, London W6 8JB

The Thorsons website address is: www.thorsons.com

Published by Thorsons 1999

5 7 9 10 8 6 4

© Herbie Brennan 1999

Herbie Brennan asserts the moral right to
be identified as the author of this work

A catalogue record for this book
is available from the British Library

ISBN 0 7225 3984 3

Printed and bound in Great Britain by
Martins the Printers Ltd, Berwick upon Tweed

INCANTATION OF LAW
AGAINST INEPT CRITICS

*Let those who read these
quatrains reflect maturely*

*Let the profane, the vulgar and the
common herd be kept away*

*Let all idiot astrologers, non-Christians
— stay distant*

*Who does otherwise, let them
be priest of the rite*

NOSTRADAMUS CENTURY 6: QUATRAIN 100

Nostradamus is the world's best-known prophet . . . and with good reason. Although the first edition of his *Centuries* was published in 1555 and the prophecies it contained often dealt with events hundreds, sometimes thousands, of years in the future, many have already come to pass.

Despite a widespread belief that Nostradamus predicted the end of the world for the year 2000, no such prophecy appears in any of his writings. The reach of his vision actually extended beyond the year 5000 AD with the human race as troubled as always, but still very much here.

In *The Little Book of Nostradamus* you will discover a special selection of those of his quatrains (four-line predictions) that seem to refer to events of our New Millennium. Keep the book in your pocket for reference. If Nostradamus again proves accurate, it contains tomorrow's news today.

When the fish of land and sea

By a great wave will be put on land

Its shape alien, smooth and horrible

By sea to the walls of the enemies soon come

CENTURY I: QUATRAIN 29

A fascinating description of military technology sometime in our future. This refers to an amphibious military vehicle capable of travelling under water. Nostradamus saw it as beached by an unexpectedly large wave on an enemy shore. If, as seems possible, the vehicle is a secret weapon, expect considerable consternation and publicity to follow its sudden appearance. (Nostradamus has more to say on this subject in the next quatrain.)

When in a fish, letters and documents
are enclosed

From out of it will come one who will then
make war

Far across the sea his fleet will have travelled

Approaching near the Italian shore

CENTURY 2: QUATRAIN 5

The 'fish' here is almost certainly a submarine – possibly even the same vehicle mentioned in the last quatrain – carrying sealed orders of a military or political nature. The distance travelled suggests a point of origin a long way from Italy, perhaps even as far as the United States.

Before battle, the great one topples

*The great one to death, death too quickly
and grieved*

Born imperfect: he goes the greater part

Near the river of blood, the earth stained

CENTURY 2: QUATRAIN 57

Although the penultimate line of the prophecy is obscure, the remainder is clear enough. It describes a time of high international tension marked by the sudden death of a high ranking politician. This may be a national statesman or President, but could equally well relate to a high United Nations official. In any case, the final line suggests the death does not avert the coming clash.

Close to Auch, Lectoure and Mirande

A great fire from heaven for three nights will fall

The cause will be seen as both amazing and miraculous

Afterwards the earth will tremble

CENTURY I: QUATRAIN 46

Scientists now estimate there are some 1,800 sizeable asteroids regularly crossing Earth's orbit while between 15 and 75 meteors strike the Earth's atmosphere every hour, so the potential for 'fire from heaven' is high. A substantial impact could well trigger earthquake activity. Auch, Lectoure and Mirande are all towns in south western France, which gives a very specific location for a rather ominous prophecy.

The great star through seven days will burn

So that two suns appear

The large mastiff all night howls

When the great pontiff changes his territory

CENTURY 2: QUATRAIN 41

This may describe the astronomical phenomenon that led to the bombardment of south west France predicted in the last quatrain. The reference to 'two suns' suggests the close approach to Earth of a fiery comet or other cosmic body. Neighbouring Italy may also be threatened by meteoric debris since the Pope will leave the Vatican to take up residence elsewhere.

Great discord shakes the land.

The agreement broken, lifting his face to heaven

The bleeding mouth swims with blood

The face anointed with milk and honey lies on the ground.

CENTURY I: QUATRAIN 57

Troubled times continue to be predicted for Northern Ireland as the Good Friday Agreement eventually shatters and bloodshed and violence become the order of the day once more. The final line is particularly interesting in that it may refer to an Orange Order banner, many of which feature depictions of King William of Orange.

Condemnation will be made of a great number

When the leaders will be reconciled

But one among them will be such bad news

That they will not remain allies for long

Although broad enough to refer to several sets of circumstances — the dispute between the Allies and the Soviets at the end of the Second World War has been mentioned — there are elements of this quatrain that, like the last, seem to fit Northern Ireland. Here Nostradamus suggests an uneasy alliance between the two sides that is eventually shattered by the behaviour of one of the individual leaders.

Before the people, blood will be spilt

From the sky it will not come

But for a long time this will not be heard

The spirit of one alone shall bear witness to it

CENTURY 9: QUATRAIN 49

A particularly interesting and unambiguous quatrain which predicts the secret execution of a popular figure, possibly by the authorities in a totalitarian State. Attempts to keep matters under wraps fail eventually due to the intervention of a witness to the atrocity. Unfortunately Nostradamus fails to pinpoint any specific location for these events.

From the rest of humanity nine will be set apart

From judgement and advice separated

Their fate will be sealed at the moment of their departure

Kappa, Theta, Lambda dead, gone, scattered

CENTURY I: QUATRAIN 81

Watch out for a hostage situation involving nine people. The mention of 'departure' suggests an air liner, ship, coach or some other form of transport. Of the nine, it seems three will perish in the crisis. Nostradamus conveniently supplies us with the initials of their names – K, T and L.

On the passing of an elderly Pope

There will be elected a Roman of good age

Who, it will be said, weakens the seat

And long held with great effort

CENTURY 5: QUATRAIN 56

Although many Popes have been elderly men at the time of their deaths and most have been Roman – or at least Italian – the fact that Nostradamus saw fit to stress the obvious here suggests an Italian Pope following a Pontiff of some other nationality – a much more rare occurrence. The incumbent at time of writing, John Paul II, is the first non-Italian Pope in 456 years and has held to traditional values with great effort. Watch out for an Italian replacement of more moderate views.

A mass of men approach from Slavonia

The Destroyer has ruined the ancient city

His Roman dream rendered desolate

He will not know how to extinguish this great flame

CENTURY 4: QUATRAIN 82

The mention of Slavonia turns our attention firmly towards the troubled Balkan States and focuses on the 'Roman dream' of Serbian expansion. The destruction of the ancient city may refer to the intensive NATO bombing campaign precipitated by the Kosovo Crisis, which Nostradamus predicts will put paid forever to nationalistic ideas of a Greater Serbia.

He who will have government of the Great Cape

Will be led to take action

The twelve Red Ones will come to spoil the cover

Under murder, murder will come to be done

CENTURY 4: QUATRAIN 11

Although frequently taken as an ecclesiastical prediction, this quatrain could as easily refer to South Africa, a country that includes Cape Province. If so, the thrust of the prophecy seems to point to an internal rebellion with considerable bloodshed before the authorities manage to restore law and order.

Before long everything will be organised

We await a sinister century

When the state of the clergy will be changed

And few will be found who want to stay in their places

CENTURY 2: QUATRAIN 10

Although non-specific, there is little doubt this prediction refers to modern times with their easy social mobility, movement towards greater and greater computer-based bureaucratic organisation and a hugely diminished role for the established Church. Nostradamus, firm supporter of conservative values, saw all these developments as 'sinister'.

Under the aquatic triplicity will be born

One who will have Thursday for his holy day

His fame, praise, rule and power will increase

By land and sea to the troubled Orient

CENTURY I: QUATRAIN 50

Watch out for the birth of a charismatic religious leader with Cancer, Scorpio and Pisces prominent in his horoscope. His new creed is predicted to spread through the industrialised West, possibly replacing established Christianity. The adoption of Thursday as a Holy Day is a little ominous. Thursday is named for Thor, the ancient Scandinavian God of Thunder.

Temples made sacred in the first Roman fashion

They will reject the deep foundations

Taking their laws first and human

Throwing out not all the cults of saints

CENTURY 2: QUATRAIN 8

The new religion predicted in the last quatrain will turn to the old pagan rites in the dedication of its temples, but adopt a hotch-potch blend of social rules and cultish practices. This is almost exactly the sort of new religion one might expect to develop as people become disenchanted with the old, since it embodied both familiar and exotic elements.

The land and air will freeze so much water

When they come to venerate Thursday

He who comes will never be so fair

Of the four quarters that honour him

CENTURY 10: QUATRAIN 71

Referring to the same events as the last two quatrains, Nostradamus shows his disapproval of the new religious leader, but also – and of far more interest – suggests all this will come to pass at a time of extreme global cooling, possibly even the onset of a new Ice Age.

The great famine which I sense approaching

Will be often turned, then become universal

So vast and long lasting that you will seize

From woods the roots and the child from the breast

CENTURY I: QUATRAIN 67

Famine, like poverty, is always with us. Nostradamus foresees an era when it will no longer be confined to poorer countries, but will spread throughout the world – a timely reminder that our current reliance on chemical fertilisers and genetic engineering may not be the whole answer.

Because of the heat of the sun on the sea

Of Ruboea, the fish are half cooked

The locals will eat them

*When in Rhodes and Genoa there will
be little food*

CENTURY 3: QUATRAIN 3

Here Nostradamus pinpoints the cause of the famine referred to in the last quatrain. If the sun has grown hot enough to half cook fish in their marine habitat, we are looking at a severe case of global warming. It seems seafood will be a welcome source of supply for a lucky few as other foodstuffs become increasingly scarce.

Populated lands will be uninhabitable

Over fields there will be great disagreement

Kingdoms given over to those incapable of prudence

Then the great brothers, Death and Dissension

CENTURY 2: QUATRAIN 95

A graphic description of the famine mentioned in the last two quatrains. As world climate changes, areas that once supported great populations become uninhabitable and the few remaining patches of arable land are subject to fierce dispute. Old governments are overthrown in favour of fanatical leaders ... with predictable results.

Earth-shaking fire from the centre of the Earth

Will make tremble all around the New City

Two great rocks will make war for a long time

Then steam will redden a new river

CENTURY I: QUATRAIN 87

It's happened often enough in movies. Now it seems New York is set for a real disaster. The 'two great rocks' at war, refers to the geological phenomenon of plate tectonics in which it is the long, slow collision of massive continental-sized rock plates that provides the trigger for earthquakes. The 'new river' may be a diversion of the Hudson, reddened by debris.

The gods will make an appearance to humans

Who will be the authors of a great conflict

Before the sky was seen free of sword and lance

On the left hand the greatest damage will
be inflicted

CENTURY 1: QUATRAIN 91

Many authors have speculated that ancient legends of meetings with 'gods' refer to visits from extra-terrestrials. If so, Nostradamus seems to be suggesting that they're on their way back . . . and humanity will follow its old habit of shooting first and asking questions afterwards. This is our first space war – with no clear indication of who is going to win.

The soulless body is no longer sacrificed

The day of death becomes the day of birth

The divine spirit will make the soul happy

Seeing the word in its eternity

CENTURY 2: QUATRAIN 13

An extensive spiritual revival is prophesied in which the old tenets of materialism fall away, and there is a widespread realisation of the immortality of consciousness and reality of reincarnation. With growing support for spiritual values provided by quantum physics, the fulfilment of this prediction may be closer than we think.

The dart of heaven will make its journey

Death spoken of, great execution

The stone in the tree, the proud nation brought down

Rumour of a human monster, purge and expiation

CENTURY 2: QUATRAIN 70

Missile strikes (which involve a great many 'darts of heaven') have become increasingly popular against those seen as human monsters, and have, in the case of Serbia, been enough to cause a capitulation. Nostradamus, with the wisdom of foresight, seems to suggest the Serbian President (still in office at time of writing) may well go too.

Great Britain, which includes England

Will be inundated as by a great flood.

The new league of Italy goes to war

So that others band against them.

One of two predictions that suggest Britain will suffer extreme flooding. (See next quatrain which also mentions Italy, at least indirectly.) The cause is not specified, but the timing is marked by the emergence of a new, more warlike Italy than we have been used to in recent years and an alliance of nations in conflict against her.

The ground trembles at Mortara

The tin island of St George half sunk

By peace made drowsy, war erupts

In the church at Easter, abyss opens

An ominous prophecy indeed, especially for British readers, since the 'tin island of St George' is clearly England. A literal interpretation suggests the disappearance of tracts of British land in an earthquake with its epicentre at Mortara in Italy, followed by war. But the sinking might be an economic slump and the war a conflict within the established Church.

Where the faint voice of woman is heard
beneath the sacred ground

A human flame shines with the divine voice

The celibates with their blood will stain the earth

And the holy temples destroyed for the
impure ones

CENTURY 4: QUATRAIN 24

Militant feminism seems ordained to solve the problem of women priests by storming the bastions of the Roman Catholic Church . . . literally. The description of the change is as violent and bloody an episode as any the Church has experienced in its long history. And ever the male chauvinist, Nostradamus cannot resist calling the new female priesthood 'impure'.

Persecuted will be the church of God

And the holy churches will be despoiled

*The child of the mother will be put naked in
a chemise*

*The Arabs will make alliance with
the Poles*

CENTURY 5: QUATRAIN 73

The third line of the quatrain suggests the Christian Church will finally acknowledge the Sacred Feminine, as the Christ child is dressed in female garb. But it happens only at a time of great persecution when, for whatever reason, staunchly Catholic Poland is joined in an alliance with one or more of the Islamic nations.

There will be heard in the sky weapons battling

During a year when religious people are enemies

They will wish the holy laws unjustly to be discussed

By lightning and war good believers are put to death

There are currently two major flash-points for wars based primarily on conflicts of religious belief – the Middle East and the India–Pakistan border. Others may arise in the future. But Nostradamus predicts coming conflicts are more likely to be resolved by aerial battles than ground troops . . . and remarks on the age-old irony that it is the good who die in religious wars.

On the establishment of the new sect

There will be found the bones of a great Roman

A marble sepulchre will be uncovered

*The earth will tremble in April, badly
buried*

58

A curiously detailed and specific prophecy relating how an earthquake, presumably in Italy, will lead to the discovery of a marble sepulchre containing the bones of an Ancient Roman of some note. The identity of the remains is not specified, nor the year when they will be discovered, but watch out for the news in April.

When the sepulchre of the great
Roman is found

The day after will be elected a Pope

By his Senate he will not be approved

Poisoned is his blood by the sacred chalice

CENTURY 3: QUATRAIN 65

Nostradamus returns to the time the marble sepulchre will be discovered with news of the election of a Pope so unpopular with the Curia that he will be poisoned using Communion wine, possibly during Mass. Whether or not he survives the attempt is not clear.

Oh great Rome, your ruin comes close

Not of your walls, but of your blood and substance

The sharp one of letters will be so horrible a notch

Pointed steel placed up his sleeve, ready to wound

CENTURY 10: QUATRAIN 65

For Nostradamus, the 'blood and substance' of Rome could only be the Catholic Church as personified in the person of the Pope. Taken as a whole, this prophecy suggests the downfall of the Church will be near when there is an assassination attempt on the Pontiff, possibly by one of his more learned Cardinals.

To a corner of the moon he will be taken

Where he will walk on foreign soil

*The unripe fruit will be the subject of
great scandal*

Great blame, but also great praise

CENTURY 9: QUATRAIN 65

Although the first two lines suggest the moon landing of 1969, the remainder of the quatrain does not fit. It may be that the manned space programme, abandoned for many years despite early successes, will be taken up again in controversial circumstances and lead to another astronaut placed on our moon.

She who was dismissed will return to reign

Her enemies found in the conspirators

More than ever will her time be triumphant

Seventy-three to death most certainly

CENTURY 6: QUATRAIN 74

Although often attributed to the reign of Queen Elizabeth I of England, there are elements in this quatrain that suggest it has yet to be fulfilled. It tells of a female ruler (not necessarily a Queen) who is deposed, then returns to lead her country to greatness ... but only after a massive purge of those who opposed her.

The Antichrist quickly annihilates three

Twenty-seven years of blood will last his war

The heretics dead, captive or exiled

Bloody corpses, water red, covering the earth

CENTURY 8: QUATRAIN 77

In a very rare direct use of the term 'Antichrist', Nostradamus forecasts more than a quarter of a century of bloody conflict before the heretical forces are finally vanquished by the legions of Christ. The reference to three annihilations is obscure. It could mean opponents, hostages or even whole countries.

An ambitious colonel engages in intrigue

And will seize the greatest army

Then mount a false insurrection against
his prince.

He will be found beneath his own flag.

CENTURY 4: QUATRAIN 62

Although often believed to refer to Cromwell, this quatrain describes a near-archetypal situation which has repeated again and again throughout history – a military coup overthrowing an existing leader and replacing him with a wholly new regime. Watch out for another turn of this familiar wheel, possibly on the African continent.

By the power of three temporal kings

To another place will the sacred throne be moved

Where the substance of the spirit body

*Will be put back and received by the
true throne*

The 'sacred throne' which to Nostradamus could only mean the Papacy was once moved from Rome to Avignon in France. Here the prophet forecasts it will be moved again, (another of his quatrains suggests to Germany). But it seems the move will lead to a spiritual renewal in the Church.

People gathered to witness something new

Princes and Kings among those present

Pillars and wall cave in, but as by a miracle

The King is saved and thirty of his onlookers

CENTURY 6: QUATRAIN 51

Although sometimes seen as the bomb plot against Hitler, this interpretation requires that terms like 'King' and 'Princes' be taken figuratively. If the quatrain is accepted literally, it may predict a disaster at the coronation of Britain's next King... but one that will spare the monarch himself.

By the shaven headed ones he will be seen
to be wrongly elected

Bowed down by a load he is unable to carry.

Such great rage and fury will he exhibit

That to fire and blood all will be reduced.

CENTURY 5: QUATRAIN 60

In an earlier book I speculated with many others that this quatrain referred to the time of the English Civil War. I now believe it deals with a wholly different time and country and predicts that the Chinese occupying Tibet will force a new 'Dalai Lama' of their own choosing on that unfortunate country. Tibetan Buddhists will not accept the imposition and a massive uprising will result.

The imitations of gold and silver inflate

And after the crime are thrown in the lake

It is discovered that all is exhausted by debt

And all scripts and bonds wiped out

A difficult quatrain in that it may predict the Great Depression of the 1930s. But the word 'crime' suggests a large-scale financial swindle was seen as the trigger, in which case the prophecy refers to a massive Stock Market crash and general economic collapse sometime in our future.

The horrible war which the West prepared

The year following will come the pestilence

So greatly horrible that neither young, old nor beast

Blood, fire, Mercury, Mars, Jupiter in France

CENTURY 9: QUATRAIN 55

More than a hint here of the use of biological weapons in a major conflict with the predictable consequences of a widespread, uncontrollable plague even after hostilities have finished. While obscure, the astrological reference in the final line suggests France may escape the worst of it.

After the pestilences have passed, the world grows small

And for a long time the lands of peace will be inhabited

People will move across the sky, the land and the sea with safety

Then wars will start again

CENTURY 1: QUATRAIN 63

Read in conjunction with the last quatrain, this one suggests that humanity will be so horrified by the result of biological warfare that it leads to an extended era of peace in which everyone can move about freely. But the idyllic situation does not last. Human nature reasserts and conflict begins again.

On the midnight hour, the army's leader

Will run away, disappearing suddenly.

Seven years later, his fame undiminished

Not once will yes be said to his return.

CENTURY 10: QUATRAIN 4

Although sometimes referred to the time of Charles II, it seems more likely that this prophecy is yet to be fulfilled. One likely candidate as the disappearing leader (at least at time of writing) is the Iraqi President Saddam Hussein who, if Nostradamus is correct, will flee opposition at home, but continue to make mischief from a base abroad as he attempts (vainly) to persuade his countrymen to invite him back.

Saturn and a water Sign in Sagittarius

In its highest increase of exaltation

Pestilence, famine, death from military hand

The century approaches its renewal

CENTURY I: QUATRAIN 16

More optimistic than it sounds at first, this prediction tells of a time suspiciously like our own. But that single word 'renewal' is a promise of better things to come as we enter the New Millennium and the New Age of Aquarius with its ancient promise of a return to more spiritual values.

Since they did not wish to consent to the divorce

Which would afterwards be seen as unworthy

The King of the Islands will be forced to abdicate

*And his place taken by another not marked out
to be King*

CENTURY 10: QUATRAIN 40

Almost universally seen as referring to the abdication of Edward VIII, the key to this quatrain is the word 'afterwards' in the second line. In his day, Wallis Simpson's divorce was always seen as unworthy, not simply in retrospect. This being so, the prediction may well refer to a time following the ascension to the British Throne of the present Prince Charles.

Twenty years of the moon's reign pass

Seven thousand years another monarch
shall hold

When the sun takes up his days

Then shall my prophecies be complete

CENTURY I: QUATRAIN 48

The quatrain that shows Nostradamus never predicted the end of the world in the year 2000.
The burn-out of the sun (line three) is still millions
of years in the future according to scientists. Even
the seven thousand years specifically mentioned in line
two will take us up to 5000 AD if dated from the birth
of Christ, 7500 AD if dated from Nostradamus' time.

Many – indeed most – of the Nostradamus prophecies are concerned with war, disease and disaster ... exactly like today's newspapers, and for much the same reason. In his visionary trances, Nostradamus was attracted to violent or emotionally-charged situations.

Taken as a whole, his *Centuries* appear superficially to predict unremitting doom and gloom, but this is no more than a trick of the prophet's perspective. History teaches us the reality of our future will be a mix of good times and bad ... exactly like our past.

About the Author

For more information on the author and his work, visit Herbie Brennan's Bookshelf on the World Wide Web at http://homepage.tinet.ie/~herbie